The

United Nations

Global Leadership

The History and Structure of the United Nations

Development and Function

by Heather Docalavich

Mason Crest Publishers

Philadelphia

Mason Crest Publishers Inc.
370 Reed Road
Broomall, Pennsylvania 19008
(866) MCP-BOOK (toll free)

First printing
1 2 3 4 5 6 7 8 9 10
              Library of Congress Cataloging-in-Publication Data

Docalavich, Heather.
  The history and structure of the United Nations : development and function / by Heather Docalavich.
      p. cm. — (The United Nations : global leadership)
  Includes bibliographical references and index.
  ISBN 1-4222-0068-X ISBN 1-4222-0065-5 (series)
  1. United Nations—History—Juvenile literature. I. Title. II. Series: United Nations—global leadership
  JZ4984.6.D63 2007
  341.23—dc22
                            2006013609

Interior design by Benjamin Stewart.
Interiors produced by Harding House Publishing Service, Inc.
www.hardinghousepages.com
Cover design by Peter Culatta.
Printed in the Hashemite Kingdom of Jordan.

Contents

Introduction
by Dr. Bruce Russett

The United Nations was founded in 1945 by the victors of World War II. They hoped the new organization could learn from the mistakes of the League of Nations that followed World War I—and prevent another war.

The United Nations has not been able to bring worldwide peace; that would be an unrealistic hope. But it has contributed in important ways to the world's experience of more than sixty years without a new world war. Despite its flaws, the United Nations has contributed to peace.

Like any big organization, the United Nations is composed of many separate units with different jobs. These units make three different kinds of contributions. The most obvious to students in North America and other democracies are those that can have a direct and immediate impact for peace.

Especially prominent is the Security Council, which is the only UN unit that can authorize the use of military force against countries and can require all UN members to cooperate in isolating an aggressor country's economy. In the Security Council, each of the big powers—Britain, China, France, Russia, and the United States—can veto any proposed action. That's because the founders of United Nations recognized that if the Council tried to take any military action against the strong opposition of a big power it would result in war. As a result, the United Nations was often sidelined during the Cold War era. Since the end of the Cold War in 1990, however, the Council has authorized many military actions, some directed against specific aggressors but most intended as more neutral peacekeeping efforts. Most of its peacekeeping efforts have been to end civil wars rather than wars between countries. Not all have succeeded, but many have. The United Nations Secretary-General also has had an important role in mediating some conflicts.

UN units that promote trade and economic development make a different kind of contribution. Some help to establish free markets for greater prosperity, or like the UN Development Programme, provide economic and technical assistance to reduce poverty in poor countries. Some are especially concerned with environmental problems or health issues. For example, the World Health Organization and UNICEF deserve great credit for eliminating the deadly disease of smallpox from the world. Poor countries especially support the United Nations for this reason. Since many wars, within and between countries, stem from economic deprivation, these efforts make an important indirect contribution to peace.

Still other units make a third contribution: they promote human rights. The High Commission for Refugees, for example, has worked to ease the distress of millions of refugees who have fled their countries to escape from war and political persecution. A special unit of the Secretary-General's office has supervised and assisted free elections in more than ninety countries. It tries to establish stable and democratic governments in newly independent countries or in countries where the people have defeated a dictatorial government. Other units promote the rights of women, children, and religious and ethnic minorities. The General Assembly provides a useful setting for debate on these and other issues.

These three kinds of action—to end violence, to reduce poverty, and to promote social and political justice—all make a contribution to peace. True peace requires all three, working together.

The UN does not always succeed: like individuals, it makes mistakes . . . and it often learns from its mistakes. Despite the United Nations' occasional stumbles, over the years it has grown and moved forward. These books will show you how.

The United Nations celebrated its fiftieth anniversary in 1995.

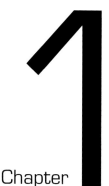

Chapter 1

Before the United Nations

Since the earliest days of recorded history, rulers of states, kingdoms, and other political bodies have negotiated with each other for the purposes of *averting* or ending military conflict. International agreements and treaties remained valid until they were rendered ineffective by subsequent violations or replaced by newer, more complicated treaties. *Alliances* were made in this way, through *negotiation*, sometimes through the exchange of *tribute*, and even through marriages. War also became an important means of defining relationships between nations, as the victors could then dictate the terms of surrender to the losers. In this way, the earliest forms of international law began to take shape.

In later times, nations followed a number of **conventions** that governed their interaction with each other. Many of these conventions were informal and could be thought of as guidelines rather than as established law. These sometimes unwritten rules dealt with everything from rules of **chivalry** on the battlefield to diplomatic **protocol**. Over time, more sophisticated systems of government began to evolve. As governments developed and began to rely more heavily on the rule of law, it became necessary to seek a common framework for resolving legal issues between and among states.

Early International Bodies

By the nineteenth century, formal alliances and organizations began to take shape. One of the first international peacekeeping organizations, the Holy Alliance, was a coalition of Russia, Austria, and Prussia created in 1815. Czar Alexander I of Russia initially proposed the alliance as a means to achieve political action through a common belief in Christianity. It became a tool for **absolute monarchs** to work together and form alliances against the rising tide of revolution and **nationalism** that was sweeping Europe.

Almost all European monarchs joined the alliance, and although there were no formal **resolutions** drafted, the diplomatic cooperation established by members of the alliance helped them to negotiate more effectively at the Congress of Vienna. The Congress of Vienna, the peace conference responsible for redrawing the political boundaries of Europe after the Napoleonic Wars, made decisions that shaped Europe as we know it today. It is also one of the earliest examples of **delegates** from several different nations coming together to create mutually binding agreements, rather than individual nations negotiating one-on-one. The Holy Alliance, however, dissolved after Czar Alexander's death in 1825.

Another important attempt by the European nations to outline specific legal obligations between countries was the First Geneva Convention. Adopted in 1864 as part of the founding of the International Red Cross, this instrument defined legal and humane treatment for battlefield casualties in wartime. The convention was inspired by the **memoirs** of a Swiss businessman, Henri Dunant, who witnessed the sufferings of soldiers wounded during a battle in 1859 between French and Austrian armies. Forty thousand soldiers on both sides were wounded in this conflict near the northern Italian town of Solferino. There was no structure in place for diplomats to arrange truces to retrieve the wounded, most of whom were left where they fell to die of their wounds or thirst. Dunant organized nearby villagers to render what aid they could, insisting on **neutrality** between

The Congress of Vienna was one of the earliest international peace conferences.

Henry Dunant, a Swiss businessman, was one of the founders of the Red Cross.

The flag of the Red Cross is an international symbol for medics in times of war.

the sides. He later wrote a book calling for the creation of a civilian relief agency to care for the wounded during wartime.

In 1863, the Geneva Society for Public Welfare became aware of the issue and created a committee of five, eventually known as the International Committee of the Red Cross. On August 22, 1864, this committee convened a meeting of **diplomats** from sixteen European countries. These diplomats ultimately created the First Geneva Convention, a treaty designed to save lives, to ease the suffering of wounded and sick soldiers, and to protect civilians who attempted to care for casualties. The conference also established an international symbol that could be used by those giving medical aid during battle. A red cross on a white field, the reverse of the Swiss flag, was chosen and is still the recognized symbol for medics in modern warfare.

The First Geneva Convention, known as the Convention for the **Amelioration** of the Condition of the Wounded in Armies in the Field, 1864, is a good example of how international law is created. Three additions followed the First Geneva Convention, and the treatment of wounded soldiers and prisoners of war has been greatly impacted by the humanitarian activities of the International Red Cross ever since. This was especially true in World War I.

World War I and the League of Nations

As World War I drew to a close, leaders on both sides were left to ponder the vast destructive power of war on a global scale. The loss of human life, as well as the loss of cities, bridges, and crops, made the total costs of such conflict nearly incalculable. The idea of creating an international body that could prevent future conflicts through negotiation was initially proposed by British foreign secretary Edward Grey, though the Democratic U.S. president Woodrow Wilson and his adviser Colonel Edward M. House ardently supported it as a means of avoiding the catastrophic loss of life seen in World War I.

The creation of such an organization became a central point of Wilson's proposal to end the war. Wilson's now-famous plan was known as the "Fourteen Points for Peace." The fourteenth point reads as follows: "A general association of nations must be formed under specific covenants for the purpose of affording mutual guarantees of political independence and territorial integrity to great and small states alike." Wilson was a strong *advocate* of including the formation of the League of Nations in the Treaty of Versailles.

On January 25, 1919, the Paris Peace Conference accepted Wilson's proposal to create the League of Nations. A special commission was formed to draft the Covenant of the League of Nations. Ultimately, the League was instituted by Part I of the Treaty of Versailles, which was signed on June 28, 1919. Forty-four different countries, including thirty-one that had taken part in the war on the side of the *Triple Entente*, signed the charter. Despite Wilson's devotion to establishing the League of Nations, the United States neither *ratified* the charter nor joined the League. However, Wilson received international acclaim for his efforts in making the League a reality, and he was awarded the Nobel Peace Prize in 1919.

The first meeting of the League was held in London on January 10, 1920, and its first official act was to ratify the Treaty of Versailles, formally ending World War I. Geneva eventually became the League's headquarters, and the first general assembly of the League was held there on November 15, 1920. Unfortunately, the League of Nations did not prove to be a long-term success. The organization met its demise with the outbreak of World War II due to a number of fundamental flaws.

Failures of the League of Nations

Like the United Nations today, the League of Nations lacked an armed force of its own and depended on the armies of member states to enforce its resolutions, which they were very reluc-

The League of Nations at its opening session in Geneva in 1920

The Palaise Wilson, headquarters of the League of Nations Secretariat from 1920 to 1936 in Geneva

tant to do. The most severe measures the League could implement outside of military action were economic **sanctions**. These were difficult to enforce and had no real effect on the sanctioned country, because it could simply trade with those nations outside the League.

The following passage, taken from *The Essential Facts About the League of Nations*, a handbook published in Geneva in 1939, illustrates the inability of the League to enforce its resolutions:

As regards the military sanctions provided for in paragraph 2 of Article 16, there is no legal obligation to apply them . . . there may be a political and moral duty incumbent on states . . . but, once again, there is no obligation on them.

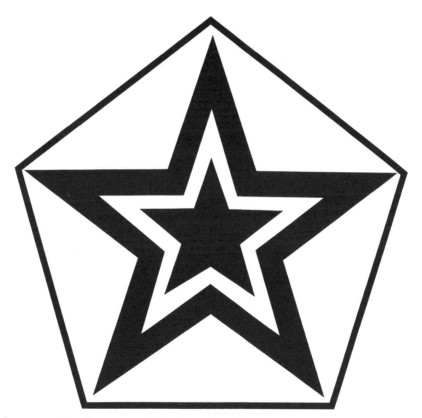

The flag flown on the League of Nations Pavilion at the New York World Exposition (1939–1941) was designed to symbolize five continents and five races.

The League's two most powerful members, Great Britain and France, were basically *pacifist* states following the bloodshed of World War I. As a result, they were extremely reluctant to use military force on behalf of the League. Both governments preferred to negotiate treaties without the involvement of the organization. In the end, Britain and France both discarded the League's philosophy of *collective security* in favor of *appeasement*, as the threat of German aggression grew with the rise to power of Adolf Hitler.

Another problem the League of Nations faced was the lack of effective representation. Although originally intended to feature representatives from all nations, many influential nations never joined or joined for only a short period of time. The fact that the United States never joined took away much of the League's potential power. Wilson was prevented from pursuing the issue when he suffered a disabling stroke.

The influence of the League was further weakened when the *fascist* nations began to leave the organization in the 1930s. Japan was originally a permanent member but saw the League as *Eurocentric* and withdrew in 1932. Italy also began as a permanent member but withdrew in 1937. The League had accepted Germany as a member in 1926, deeming it a "peace-loving country" rehabilitated from its involvement in World War I. However, Adolf Hitler withdrew Germany from membership when he came to power in 1933. The Soviet Union was only a member from 1934 to December 14, 1939, when it was expelled for hostile action against Finland.

The League's neutrality looked a lot like indecision. The League required unanimous agreement to enact a resolution, so taking quick and effective action was difficult, if not impossible. This combination of weaknesses left the League ill-equipped to effectively prevent the outbreak of World War II.

The Creation of the United Nations

Following the League's failure to prevent World War II, the nations of the world decided to create a new organization to fulfill the League's role. This body eventually became the United Nations. Many agencies initially connected to the League of Nations, for instance the International Labour Organisation, continued to function and eventually became associated with the United Nations. At a meeting of the assembly in 1946, the League of Nations dissolved itself, and all of its services, mandates, and property were transferred to the newly formed United Nations.

The warfare of World War II inspired the world's nations to try again to form an international peacekeeping organization.

The Declaration by the United Nations was signed in 1942.

The structure of the United Nations was designed to make it more effective than the League. The Allied forces of World War II (Britain, the Soviet Union, France, the United States, and China) became permanent members of the UN Security Council. Decisions of the UN Security Council are binding on all members of the United Nations. However, unlike the League of Nations, unanimous decisions are not required.

Like the League of Nations, the United Nations does not have its own armies, but the organization has been more effective than the League in calling for its members to contribute to missions requiring military force. Examples of such UN missions include the Korean War and peacekeeping efforts in the former Yugoslavia. The United Nations also relies on economic sanctions to enforce its resolutions. Here again, the United Nations has been more successful than the League in attracting members from all corners of the world, giving its sanctions more force. Finally, after decades of negotiation and the hard-won experiences gained through bloody conflict, the international community was able to convene an international body of real significance.

Churchill, Roosevelt, and Stalin at the Atlantic Charter meeting in 1941

Chapter 2

Purposes and Principles: The UN Charter

We the peoples of the United Nations determined to save succeeding generations from the scourge of war, which twice in our lifetime has brought untold sorrow to mankind, and to reaffirm faith in fundamental human rights, in the dignity and worth of the human person, in the equal rights of men and women and of nations large and small, and to establish conditions under which justice and respect for the obligations arising from treaties and other sources of international law can be maintained, and to promote social progress and better standards of life in larger freedom, and for these ends to practice tolerance and live together in peace with one another as good neighbours, and to unite our strength to maintain international peace and security, and to ensure, by the acceptance of principles and the institution of methods, that armed force shall not be used, save in the common interest, and to employ international machinery for the promotion of the economic and social advancement of all peoples, have resolved to combine our efforts to accomplish these aims. Accordingly, our respective Governments, through representatives assembled in the city of San Francisco, who have exhibited their full powers found to be in good and due form, have agreed to the present Charter of the United Nations and do hereby establish an international organization to be known as the United Nations.

We the peoples of the United ⊕ Nation

We the peoples

Determined

to save succeeding generations from the scourge of war, which twice in our lifetime has brought untold sorrow to mankind, **and to** reaffirm faith in fundamental human rights, in the dignity and worth of the human person, in the equal rights of men and women and of nations large and small, **and to** establish conditions under which justice and respect for the obligations arising from treaties and other sources of international law can be maintained, **and to** promote social progress and better standards of life in larger freedom,

And for these ends

to practice tolerance and live together in peace with one another as good neighbours, **and to** unite our strength to maintain international peace and security, **and to** ensure, by the acceptance of principles and the institution of methods, that armed force shall not be used, save in the common interest, **and to** employ international machinery for the promotion of the economic and social advancement of all peoples,

Have resolved to combine our efforts to accomplish these aims

Accordingly, our respective Governments, through representatives assembled in the ci of San Francisco, who have exhibited their full powers found to be in good and due for have agreed to the present Charter of the United Nations and do hereby establish an international organization to be known as t United Nations.

Preamble to the Charter of the United Nations
Published by the United Nations Department of Public Informa
Photographs and Exhibits Section.

The preamble of the UN Charter

Chapter Two—Purposes and Principles: The UN Charter

The passage above is the ***preamble*** to the UN Charter, the constitution of the United Nations that is loosely based on the Constitution of the United States. This important document was signed by fifty of the fifty-one original member countries at the United Nations Conference on International Organization in San Francisco on June 26, 1945 (although it did not attend the San Francisco conference, Poland did later sign the document and is considered one of the original members). The five founding members (the Republic of China, France, the Soviet Union, the United Kingdom, and the United States) then ratified it, as did a majority of the other ***signatories***. It entered into force on October 24, 1945. The United States was the third country to join the new international organization, after Nicaragua and El Salvador.

The charter is comprised of the preamble and a series of chapters made up of the various articles. The document acts as a type of treaty, and all member nations are obligated to abide by the articles it contains. The articles of the charter are also meant to ***supersede*** all other treaties to which member nations may be party.

The UN Charter: Chapter by Chapter

Each chapter of the UN Charter describes a particular area of international law and the obligations of each member nation in regard to that area of the law. The structure and function of the different bodies of the United Nations are also described here.

Chapter I establishes the overall goals of the United Nations as an organization. These include important provisions for the preservation of international peace and security. The text of Article 1 of Chapter I states the following:

> The Purposes of the United Nations are:
> - To maintain international peace and security, and to that end: to take effective collective measures for the prevention and removal of threats to the peace, and for the suppression of acts of aggression or other breaches of the peace, and to bring about by peaceful means, and in conformity with the principles of justice and international law, adjustment or settlement of international disputes or situations which might lead to a breach of the peace;
> - To develop friendly relations among nations based on respect for the principle of equal rights and self-determination of peoples, and to take other appropriate measures to strengthen universal peace;
> - To achieve international co-operation in solving international problems of an eco-

nomic, social, cultural, or humanitarian character, and in promoting and encouraging respect for human rights and for fundamental freedoms for all without distinction as to race, sex, language, or religion; and

- To be a centre for harmonizing the actions of nations in the attainment of these common ends.

Thus, Chapter I declares the United Nations to be an international body concerned not only with matters of war and peace but also with all aspects of international cooperation. In addition to describing the purposes of the body as a whole, Article 2 lists the obligations of member nations, whose conduct must be in accordance with these purposes. It is expected that member nations will be committed to the peaceful resolution of disputes and that the United Nations will use its influence on nonmember nations to persuade them to live in peace.

Chapter II deals with the qualifications for membership in the United Nations. All signatories of the charter are declared to be original members. In addition, Article 4 defines the criteria for nations wishing to apply for membership: "Membership in the United Nations is open to all other

The UN's first General Assembly in 1946

The second through the fifth sessions of the General Assembly were held in Flushing Meadows, New York.

An early United Nations conference in New York City

peace-loving states which accept the obligations contained in the present charter and, in the judgment of the Organization, are able and willing to carry out these obligations." The charter also requires membership decisions to be made by the General Assembly on the recommendation of the Security Council. Chapter II also outlines provisions for the suspension of member states from the United Nations. The Security Council can vote to revoke the membership privileges of member nations. Nations can also be expelled from the organization. As with membership, this is done by vote of the General Assembly, with the recommendation of the Security Council.

Chapters III through XV, the majority of the document, describe the various bodies of the United Nations, as well as their respective functions and areas of authority. The principle bodies established by Chapter III include a General Assembly, a Security Council, an Economic and Social Council, a Trusteeship Council, an International Court of Justice, and a Secretariat. The chapters that follow provide an in-depth description of the powers of each body. They also establish that men and women should have an equal right to participate in all of these bodies.

Chapters XVI and XVII describe the procedure for integrating UN policies with established international law. In Chapter XVI, Article 103 states, "In the event of a conflict between the obligations of the Members of the United Nations under the present Charter and their obligations under any other international agreement, their obligations under the present Charter shall prevail." Chapter XVII also reaffirms the treaties made to end World War II. Chapters XVIII and XIX provide for ratification of the charter and provisions for making *amendments*.

The final and perhaps most important chapters describe the enforcement powers of UN bodies. Chapter VI describes the Security Council's power to investigate and resolve conflicts; Chapter VII describes the Security Council's power to authorize economic, diplomatic, and military sanctions, as well as the use of military force, to resolve disputes; Chapters IX and X describe the UN's responsibilities in regard to economic and social cooperation, and the powers of the Economic and Social Council; Chapters XII and XIII describe the Trusteeship Council, which administered *decolonization*; and Chapters XIV and XV describe the powers of, respectively, the International Court of Justice and the UN Secretariat.

A Living Document

Even as the charter was being written, all parties were aware that in order for their infant organization to succeed, the charter would need the flexibility to adapt to the needs of its growing membership and an ever-changing world. For this reason, the charter established a procedure to make

Eleanor Roosevelt, President Roosevelt's wife, made sure that women were involved in the United Nations' work.

amendments. Five different amendments have been made to the UN Charter since it first came into force.

An amendment to Article 23 was adopted by the General Assembly on December 17, 1963, and came into force on August 31, 1965. This amendment enlarged the membership of the Security Council from eleven to fifteen. Article 27 and Article 61 were also amended at that time. Article 27 was amended to require that decisions of the Security Council on all matters would be made by an affirmative vote of nine members instead of seven, including the concurring votes of the five permanent members of the Security Council. The amendment to Article 61 enlarged the membership of the Economic and Social Council from eighteen to twenty-seven. A second amendment to that Article, which entered into force on September 24, 1973, further increased the membership of the Council from twenty-seven to fifty-four.

An amendment to Article 109 adopted by the General Assembly on December 20, 1965, came into force on June 12, 1968. The amendment, which relates to the first paragraph of that article, states that a General Conference of Member States may be held at a date and place to be determined by a two-thirds vote of the members of the General Assembly and by a vote of any nine members (formerly seven) of the Security Council. Such a conference would be held for the purpose of reviewing the charter. Originally, the charter provided for a review conference to be held in 1955, during the organization's tenth session.

The charter provides a solid basis for the United Nations to function as an influential body of real international importance. The document not only gives a clear description of the organization's goals, subsidiary bodies, and their functions, but it also is the structure through which the United Nations can adapt to the constantly changing dynamics of global affairs.

The secretary-general and the chief architect seal the UN building's cornerstone.

Chapter **3**

The United Nations: Policy-Making Bodies and Their Functions

T he UN General Assembly is one of the six principal organs of the United Nations, and it is its primary policy-making body. It is made up of all UN member states and meets in annual sessions under a president elected from among the representatives. The first session was convened in London on January 10, 1946, and included representatives of fifty-one nations.

The regular session is usually convened on the third Tuesday in September and ends in mid-December of every year. Special sessions can be called by the Security Council, a majority of UN members, or, if the majority agrees, by a single member. Such a special session was held in September 2005 to commemorate the organization's sixtieth anniversary; the session was used to discuss progress on the UN's Millennium Development Goals and to discuss Kofi Annan's "In Larger Freedom" plan.

Structure of the General Assembly

Voting in the General Assembly on most issues is determined by a two-thirds majority of those present and voting. Issues requiring a two-thirds majority include recommendations on peace and security; election of members to the UN's principal organs; admission, suspension, and expulsion of members; and budgetary matters. Other questions are decided by a simple majority vote. Each member country has one vote.

Except for budgetary matters, General Assembly resolutions are not binding on the members. Assembly resolutions are basically recommendations, or statements of general opinion, rather than binding international law. The General Assembly can address any matters within the boundaries of the UN's Charter, except matters of peace and security under Security Council consideration.

The General Assembly serves as an important forum for members to launch initiatives on international questions of security, economic development, and human rights. This forum is critical because the assembly is the only organ of the United Nations where all member countries are represented, regardless of size, wealth, or influence.

If the Security Council is unable, due to disagreement among the permanent members, to exercise its primary responsibility, the General Assembly may take action on issues regarding peace and security. Adopted in 1950, a series of resolutions known as the "Uniting for Peace" resolutions, empower the General Assembly to meet in an emergency session to recommend action in the case of an act of aggression. Two-thirds of the members must approve any such recommendation.

During the 1980s, the General Assembly became a place to discuss differences between the world's industrialized nations and developing countries. These issues gained importance on the international stage because of the phenomenal growth and changing makeup of UN membership.

In contrast to 1945, when the United Nations had fifty-one members, it now has 191, of which more than two-thirds are developing countries. Having gained strength in numbers, developing

Trygve Lie of Norway was the United Nations' first secretary-general.

This boy, a refugee of World War II, was one of those who benefited from the United Nations' work.

countries are now often able to establish the agenda of the General Assembly, define the nature of its debates, and impact its decisions. For many developing countries, the United Nations is the source of much of their international relevance and a principal diplomatic outlet.

The Security Council

The Security Council is the most dominant organ of the United Nations. Maintaining peace and security between nations is its foremost responsibility. While other UN bodies can only make suggestions to member governments, the Security Council has the power to make decisions that member governments are obligated to comply with under the UN Charter.

Decisions of the Council are called Security Council Resolutions. Security Council members must always be present at UN headquarters so it can meet on a moment's notice to address an

First meeting of the Security Council

emergency situation; the charter made this requirement to address the inability of the old League of Nations to respond rapidly to a crisis. The presidency of the Security Council is rotated and lasts for one month. The president sets the agenda, presides over meetings, and oversees any crises. The presidency rotates according to the alphabetical order of the members' names in English. The Security Council is comprised of permanent members and temporary members.

Permanent Members

The original permanent members of the Security Council were the victorious Allied forces of World War II. In 1971, the People's Republic of China replaced the Republic of China as China's representative to the United Nations. In 1991, Russia became the successor to the seat originally held by the Soviet Union, including the seat in the Security Council. Each permanent member also has the authority to void any resolution, with a single blocking vote that outweighs any majority.

At present, only the five permanent members are legally permitted to possess nuclear weapons under the Nuclear Non-Proliferation Treaty. Unfortunately, the treaty lacks ***universal validity***, as not all nuclear nations are parties to the treaty. India, Pakistan, and allegedly, Israel all possess nuclear weapons outside the provisions of the treaty. It is also believed that other countries such as North Korea and Iran are working to develop nuclear arms; thus the ability of the Security Council to prevent nuclear conflict is somewhat diminished as more and more countries seek nuclear weaponry.

Temporary Members

Ten temporary Security Council members are elected by the General Assembly for two-year terms starting on January 1, with five replaced each year. These members are chosen by region and confirmed by the General Assembly. The African nations choose three members; the Latin American, Asian, and Western European nations choose two members each; and the Eastern European bloc chooses one member.

In recent years, there has been a movement to increase the number of permanent members on the Security Council. Japan, India, and Germany have all made persuasive arguments for being included as members. Japan and Germany are the second and third largest sources of funding to the United Nations. Meanwhile, India and Germany contribute the most troops to UN peacekeeping missions of any other nations.

One proposed solution is to increase the number of permanent members to eleven. The

Meeting of the Security Council in 1995

The first summit-level meeting of the Security Council

The United Nations worked to bring peace in Southeast Asia during the 1970s. Here, a child stands in front of the Killing Fields memorial in Phnom Penh.

expanded Security Council would then include Japan, Germany, India, and Brazil as permanent members and include two new permanent members from Africa, most likely South Africa and Egypt. Currently, this proposal has to be accepted by two-thirds of the General Assembly, which translates to 128 votes.

Structure of the Security Council

Most decisions made by the Security Council require an affirmative vote by nine or more members. A veto by any permanent member of the council prevents adoption of a resolution, even if it has received nine or more affirmative votes. Countries may also choose to ***abstain*** from a vote; abstention is not regarded as a veto. Since the Security Council's inception, China has used five vetoes; France, eighteen; Russia/USSR, 122; the United Kingdom, thirty-two; and the United States, seventy-nine. Nations who are not members of the Security Council may be invited to take part in Security Council discussions if their interests may be affected by the outcome of the debate.

A meeting of the Economic and Social Council in New York in 1982

The Security Council "may investigate any dispute, or any situation which might lead to international friction or give rise to a dispute" under Chapter VI of the UN Charter. It may also "recommend appropriate procedures or methods of adjustment" if it feels there is a threat to global peace and security. Such recommendations are not binding on UN members.

When situations arise that pose "threats to the peace, breaches of the peace, or acts of aggression," the Security Council has broader authority. In such situations, it has several options for action, including the use of armed force "to maintain or restore international peace and security" under Chapter VII of the UN Charter. Chapter VII provided the basis for UN military action in 1950 during the Korean War and the use of coalition forces in Iraq and Kuwait in 1991. All actions taken under Chapter VII, such as economic sanctions, are legally binding on UN members.

The Economic and Social Council

The Economic and Social Council (ECOSOC) of the United Nations assists the General Assembly in promoting economic and social development between nations. The ECOSOC has fifty-four members, eighteen of whom are elected each year by the General Assembly to a three-year term. All decisions are made by a majority of the members present and voting, and each member has one vote. The ECOSOC meets annually in July for a four-week session. Beginning in 1998, it has held a second meeting each April with finance ministers who run important committees of the World Bank and the International Monetary Fund.

A separate entity from the many specialized bodies it coordinates, the ECOSOC's functions include gathering information, advising member nations, and making recommendations. It is also well suited to provide consistency in developing policy and coordinating the functions of the UN's *subsidiary* bodies. Historically, the ECOSOC has served principally as a forum for discussion of economic and social issues; it had little real authority. However, beginning in 1992, an effort was made to make the ECOSOC more relevant by strengthening its responsibilities in economic, social, and related fields, particularly in advancing development goals.

These changes made the ECOSOC the oversight and policy-setting body for UN operational development activities and created smaller executive boards for the UN Development Programme (UNDP), UN Population Fund (UNFPA), and UN Children's Fund (UNICEF), which would provide those agencies with operating guidance and facilitate better management. The reform also gave the ECOSOC more power to ensure that UN agencies coordinated their work on issues of common interest, such as narcotics control, human rights, the reduction of poverty, and the prevention of HIV/AIDS.

The Trusteeship Council met in New York in 1992.

One positive impact of this reform was the ECOSOC decision in 1994 to authorize the creation of a new joint and cosponsored UN program on HIV/AIDS. This program (UNAIDS) will bring together previously established AIDS-related resources and give them access to the expertise of the World Health Organization, as well as the combined resources of UNICEF, UNDP, UNFPA, UNESCO, and the World Bank. By creating one consolidated global program, the ECOSOC eliminated the duplication of efforts and enhanced the ability of member states to cope with the AIDS *pandemic*. It began operating in January 1996.

The Trusteeship Council

The UN Trusteeship Council is the last of the principal organs of the United Nations. Its mission was to help ensure that territories under foreign rule were governed in the best interests of the inhabitants and of international peace and security. The trust territories—mostly former colonial holdings—have all now attained self-government or independence, either as separate nations or by joining neighboring countries. The last such nation was Palau, which became a member of the United Nations in December 1994.

Its mission fulfilled, the Trusteeship Council suspended its operation on November 1, 1994, and although under the UN Charter it continues to exist on paper, its future role and even existence remain uncertain. However, formal elimination of the Trusteeship Council would require the revision of the UN Charter.

In a 1996 report titled "Our Global Neighborhood," the Commission on Global Governance recommended amending Chapters XII and XIII of the UN Charter to give the Trusteeship Council authority over the oceans, the atmosphere, outer space, and Antarctica. Soon afterward, the World Federalist Movement, an international nongovernmental organization with a consultative status with the ECOSOC and committed to reforming the United Nations and ensuring effective democratic global governance, issued an action alert calling for members to *lobby* their governments in support of this reform. Although many environmentalists agree that an international regulatory body should be employed to protect areas outside national jurisdictions, the United Nations has not shown much enthusiasm for the idea. In March 2005, UN Secretary-General Kofi Annan proposed the complete elimination of the Trusteeship Council as part of his proposed reforms.

The International Court of Justice is in The Hague in the Netherlands.

Chapter 4

The UN's Judicial Organ: The International Court of Justice

The International Court of Justice (ICJ), often called simply "the World Court," is the main judicial organ of the United Nations. Established by the UN Charter, its main responsibilities are to settle conflicts submitted to it by member nations and to give advisory opinions on questions submitted to it by the General Assembly, the Security Council, or by other UN agencies. This court is different from the International Criminal Court, which is often confused with the International Court of Justice.

Structure of the Court

The ICJ is headquartered in The Hague, the Netherlands. Its fifteen judges are elected by the UN General Assembly and the UN Security Council from a list of persons nominated by national groups. Judges serve for nine years and may be reelected. No two judges may be citizens of the same country. One-third of the ICJ is elected every three years. Each of the five permanent members of the Security Council always has a judge on the ICJ.

Questions before the ICJ are decided by a majority of judges present. The UN Charter states that in arriving at its decisions, the ICJ shall apply international conventions, international custom, and the "general principles of law recognized by civilized nations." It can also refer to academic writing and previous judicial **precedent** to help interpret the law, although the ICJ is not required to abide by its previous decisions. If the parties agree, the ICJ may also rule *ex aequo et bono,* or "in justice and fairness." This means that the ICJ may make a decision based on general ideas of fairness rather than specific law.

The ICJ rules on two different types of cases: states may agree to be bound by the ruling of the court when there is an issue of **contention** between them that they would like to have resolved; the ICJ also issues advisory opinions, which provide advice on questions of international law, usually submitted by the UN General Assembly. Several international treaties go so far as to name the ICJ as the authority in disputes over interpretation and application of the agreement.

Contentious Issues

Contentious cases before the ICJ always involve conflicts between nations. The ICJ can only rule in cases where both parties have agreed to bring the matter before the court. If either country fails "to perform the obligations **incumbent** upon it under a judgment rendered by the Court," the Security Council may be called on to "make recommendations or decide upon measures." The Security Council must vote to decide on what action, if any, is warranted.

Unfortunately, the ICJ has historically been weakened by an unwillingness of the losing party to be bound by its ruling, and by the Security Council's unwillingness to enforce consequences. According to the law, however, "so far as the parties to the case are concerned, a judgment of the Court is binding, final and without appeal," and "by signing the Charter, a State Member of the United Nations undertakes to comply with any decision of the International Court of Justice in a case to which it is a party."

One example is a case called *Nicaragua v. United States.* The United States had previously

The International Court of Justice building

The ICJ wanted to ensure that nuclear war would never again threaten the people of the world.

acknowledged the ICJ's jurisdiction on its creation in 1946 but withdrew its acceptance following a ruling in 1984 that called on the United States to "cease and to refrain" from the "unlawful use of force" against the government of Nicaragua. The ICJ ruled the United States was "in **breach** of its obligation under customary international law not to use force against another state" and ordered the United States to pay **reparations**. The United States decided not to pay, stating that the ICJ lacked jurisdiction to rule in the case.

Critics often point to the ICJ's unwillingness to take on politically controversial cases. Because the ICJ has no real power to enforce its rulings, its survival is dependent on its political relevance—and that would be endangered if its rulings were constantly ignored by member states. This unwillingness to take on controversial issues is viewed as one of the ICJ's major shortcomings.

Advisory Opinions

The ICJ provides advisory opinions only to specific UN bodies and agencies. When considering a request, the ICJ decides which nations and organizations might provide useful information and gives them an opportunity to present written or oral briefings. The ICJ's advisory procedure is otherwise based on that for contentious proceedings, and the sources of international law are the same. Advisory opinions are considered more as recommendations than as rulings. As a result, they do not generally aim to resolve specific controversies. Certain resolutions or treaties can, however, state in advance that the advisory opinion will be binding on particular agencies or states. Some courts, including federal courts in the United States, are constitutionally forbidden from issuing advisory opinions, but Article 65, paragraph 1 of the Statute of the International Court of Justice expressly authorizes the ICJ to render advisory opinions.

In short, advisory opinions of the court are significant and widely respected interpretations of the law, but they are not enforceable, and they are essentially nonbinding under the Statute of the Court. An example of a past advisory opinion is "The Advisory Opinion of the International Court of Justice of July 8, 1996." This opinion provides one of the few authoritative judicial decisions concerning the legality of the use of nuclear weapons under international law.

In this opinion, the ICJ decided unanimously that any threat of the use of force, or the actual use of force, by means of nuclear weapons that is contrary to Article 2, paragraph 4 of the UN Charter is unlawful. The ICJ also stated that the threat or use of nuclear weapons would generally be against the rules of international law applicable in armed conflict, and would violate the principles and rules governing **humanitarian** law. Nonetheless, the ICJ's opinion did not conclude,

The ICJ works to provide justice to the entire world.

under the existing state of international law at the time, that in an extreme circumstance of self-defense where the very survival of a country would be at stake, the threat or use of nuclear weapons would necessarily be unlawful in all possible cases.

In a unanimous finding, the ICJ further agreed that any threat or use of nuclear weapons would need to meet all requirements of international law relating to armed conflict, chiefly the principles and rules of international humanitarian law, and would also need to comply with specific obligations under treaties and other undertakings that expressly deal with nuclear weapons. In its final declaration, the ICJ decided unanimously that there exists an obligation to actively pursue nuclear disarmament in all its aspects under strict international control.

UN headquarters in New York City

The UN's Administrative and Executive Body: The Secretariat

"I am a cheerleader, I am a promoter, I am a salesman, I am a debt collector, I am a father confessor and there are other aspects I still have to discover," said Kofi Annan, UN secretary-general, of his job.

The UN Secretariat is a principal organ of the United Nations, headed by the UN secretary-general. A staff of international civil servants stationed throughout the world assists the secretary-general. The Secretariat provides studies, information, and facilities needed by UN bodies for their meetings. Basically the executive arm of the UN system, the Secretariat carries out tasks as directed by the UN Security Council, the UN General Assembly, the UN Economic and Social Council, and other UN bodies. The UN Charter demands that the staff be chosen by application of the "highest standards of efficiency, competence, and integrity," with special attention paid to the importance of recruiting on a wide geographical basis.

How the Secretariat Operates

The UN Charter provides that the staff shall not take advice or direction from any authority other than the United Nations. Member nations respect this aspect of the secretariat and should not seek to influence its members. The secretary-general alone chooses the staff and is responsible for maintaining a pool of talented individuals from all across the globe.

The secretary-general works to resolve international disputes, administers peacekeeping operations, arranges for international conferences, does research for the implementation of Security Council decisions, and consults with member governments regarding various programs. Main Secretariat offices in this area include the Office of the Coordinator of Humanitarian Affairs and the Department of Peacekeeping Operations. The secretary-general may draw to the attention of the Security Council any issue that, in his or her opinion, may threaten international peace and security.

As the UN's "chief administrative officer," the secretary-general has an important role to play

UN Secretaries-General

Trygve Lie (Norway) February 1946–November 1952
Dag Hammarskjöld (Sweden) April 1953–September 1961
U Thant (Burma, now Myanmar) November 1961–December 1971
Kurt Waldheim (Austria) January 1972–December 1981
Javier Pérez de Cuéllar (Peru) January 1982–December 1991
Boutros Boutros-Ghali (Egypt) January 1992–December 1996
Kofi Annan (Ghana) January 1997–present

Dag Hammarskjold of Sweden was the second secretary-general.

Secretary-General Hammarskjold in the Congo in 1960

Secretary-General Hammarskjold inspecting a UN battalion

in international affairs. The position was initially designed to be purely administrative. However, Trygve Lie, the first secretary-general, set a precedent when he chose to magnify his responsibilities and act as a world leader and mediator. Every secretary-general to follow him has spoken out on global issues and worked to maintain peace through mediation.

Term and Selection of the Secretary-General

The secretary-general is elected to a five-year term. Traditionally, each secretary-general serves two terms in office. By convention, the position of secretary-general rotates by geographic region. An exception to this rule was made with the selection of Kofi Annan. When Boutros Boutros-Ghali of Egypt served only one term, another African, Kofi Annan of Ghana, was chosen to succeed him. When Annan had finished his first term, member states were so impressed with his performance that he was selected for a second term despite the fact that it was now time to select a candidate from Asia. There has never been a secretary-general from North America.

U Thant of Burma was the United Nations' third secretary-general.

Chapter Five—The UN's Administrative and Executive Body: The Secretariat

Most secretaries-general come from medium-sized countries or "middle powers" with little prior fame. Although high-profile candidates are frequently mentioned as next in line for the job, these are almost always rejected. Examples of such figures who were rejected for the post include Charles de Gaulle, Dwight Eisenhower, and Anthony Eden, all rejected in favor of the little known Norwegian Trygve Lie.

Recently, Secretary-General Kofi Annan proposed several reforms for the Secretariat. These planned changes include appointing a scientific adviser, creating a peace-building support office, establishing a cabinet-style panel for decision making, and strengthening the Secretariat's role as a mediator. He also called for several administrative and budgetary reforms, and pointed out the need to "to review all mandates older than five years to see whether the activities concerned are still genuinely needed or whether the resources assigned to them can be reallocated in response to new and emerging challenges."

The Seventh Secretary-General

Kofi Atta Annan, a Ghanaian diplomat, was born April 8, 1938, to Henry Reginald and Victoria Annan in Kumasi, Ghana. As is common in the Akan language, he was named to indicate his birthday and place in his family: Kofi means a boy born on Friday, and Annan represents the fourth child of the family. Annan was a twin, an occurrence that is regarded as important in Ghanaian culture.

Annan's family was part of the Ghanian elite; both of his grandfathers and his uncle were influential chiefs. His father was half Asante and half Fante; his mother was Fante. Annan's father was a prosperous export manager for a cocoa company. In his youth, Annan attended the elite Mfantsipim School, a Methodist boarding school in Cape Coast founded in the 1870s. There, Annan learned "that suffering anywhere concerns people everywhere." Ghana became the first British colony in sub-Saharan Africa to gain independence in 1957, the year Annan graduated from Mfantsipim.

The next year, Annan returned to his hometown and began studying for a degree in economics at the Kumasi College of Science and Technology, now the University of Science and Technology. He applied for and received a Ford Foundation grant, which enabled him to travel to the United States and complete his undergraduate studies at Macalester College in St. Paul, Minnesota. Annan then studied at the Graduate Institute of International Studies in Geneva, Switzerland, from 1961 to 1962, later attending the MIT Sloan School of Management from 1971 to 1972 as a Sloan Fellow and receiving a Master of Science degree in management with a minor

Kofi Annan

in poetry. An accomplished linguist, Annan is fluent in English, French, several dialects of Akan, and other African languages.

Annan began his career working for the World Health Organization in 1962. He returned home to work as Ghana's director of tourism, a position he held from 1974 to 1976. Following that, he went back to work for the United Nations as an assistant secretary-general in three different positions. He worked as human resources management and security coordinator from 1987 to 1990, program planning, budget and finance, and controller from 1990 to 1992, and managed peacekeeping operations from March 1993 to February 1994. Annan was then an undersecretary-general until October 1995, when he was named a special representative of the secretary-general to the former Yugoslavia, serving for five months in this position before returning to his duties as undersecretary-general in April 1996.

Annan was selected by the UN Security Council to be secretary-general on December 13, 1996, and was confirmed four days later by the General Assembly. He began his first term as secretary-general on January 1, 1997, when he replaced outgoing Secretary-General Boutros Boutros-Ghali of Egypt. Annan was the first person from a black African nation to become secretary-general.

He issued a five-point "Call to Action" in April 2001 to address the HIV/AIDS epidemic. Annan has made the fight against this epidemic his "personal priority" as secretary-general and in life in general. He proposed the creation of a global AIDS and health fund to encourage increased spending needed to help developing countries battle the HIV/AIDS crisis. On December 10, 2001, Annan and the United Nations jointly received the Nobel Peace Prize, "for their work for a better organized and more peaceful world."

Chapter **6**

Financing the
United Nations

The United Nations and all its agencies and funds spend about $10 billion each year; that's about $1.70 for each man, woman, and child on the Earth. This is a very small figure compared to most national budgets, and it is just a tiny fraction of the world's total defense spending. Yet for over a decade, the United Nations has faced a crippling financial crisis and been forced to eliminate many important programs in several areas.

Mothers and children in the Congo received vaccinations, thanks to the United Nations. Efforts like these cost money.

Many proposals for UN reform deal with reorganizing its funding system. Some suggest that the United Nations must seek alternative means to fund its programs. Proposed alternatives include establishing a global tax on currency transactions, environmental taxes, and taxes on the arms trade. However, member nations responsible for the highest contributions are hesitant to reform the system for fear they could lose political influence.

The Assessment System

The United Nations funds its programs through a system of assessments by which each member nation is billed for its membership according to a specific formula. This formula determines each member's assessed share of the UN regular and peacekeeping budgets based on the principle of relative ability to pay, calculated from a ten-year average of each country's ***gross domestic product***, with reductions made for low ***per capita income*** and high foreign debt.

According to this formula, the United States, which has the world's largest economy, is also the largest contributor to the UN budget. However, many member states have not paid their full dues and have cut their donations to the UN's voluntary funds. Sometimes they refuse to pay a portion of their dues, citing that the money would be used to support this or that program to which they are opposed. As of December 31, 2004, funds owed in ***arrears*** to the UN Regular Budget topped $357 million, of which the United States alone owed $241 million. This has combined with other factors to create a severe financial crisis for the United Nations.

History of the Crisis

The United Nations has faced financial difficulties from its earliest years. Members paid late or fell into arrears. But the first true financial crises arose over early peacekeeping operations. In 1956, the first major peacekeeping operation in the Sinai set off a dispute over who should pay, since there was no clear precedent. Several states refused to pay their share, some on the grounds that those responsible for the crisis should bear the cost. In the 1960s, a large and divisive peacekeeping operation in the Congo led a number of countries again to withhold payments because they disagreed with the action. The Congo mission was by far the most expensive ever mounted, so it set off an especially serious financial crisis. The Soviet Union, with its relatively large assessment, led the list of UN debtors.

The General Assembly resolved the Congo financial crisis by authorizing a UN bond issue to cover unpaid assessments. Altogether, the United Nations issued $169 million in bonds in the

1960s. The UN later paid off the bonds from regular assessment income. In turn, some countries then withheld **_prorated_** sums from their assessments, refusing to pay the portion of their assessment that would go to bond service. The end of the 1960s had established two unwritten rules: First, countries could withhold all or part of their assessed payments because of policy disputes. And second, countries could reduce their regular budget payments through targeted "withholdings."

To ease the financial strain, the General Assembly approved a plan to delay payment to countries supplying troops and equipment to peacekeeping operations. This meant that the United Nations essentially forced a loan onto these countries, some of them smaller or poor nations. In 1965, members were invited to contribute to a special account that acted as a reserve fund, expanding on another small fund set up in 1945. These two funds provided the United Nations with a small financial cushion. However, this would still prove to be inadequate to meet the needs of the growing organization.

Children in Senegal go to school because of UN funding.

A UN peacekeeper with a child in the Congo; the UN mission to the Congo was one of its most expensive, setting off a financial crisis for the United Nations.

The Gulf War was expensive for the United States.

American warfare uses up U.S. dollars, leaving little left to support the United Nations' more peaceful missions.

During this period, the United States paid its dues and peacekeeping assessments. By the 1980s, though, feelings in Washington had changed about the fairness of UN assessments. In 1983, the United States began to deny funding to UN programs that supported the Palestine Liberation Organization or SWAPO, an independence movement in Namibia. U.S. arrears continued to climb as the decade progressed, jumping from $12 million in 1984 to $86 million in 1985, forcing the United Nations to cut spending by 10 percent and lay off many staff.

By the end of the first Gulf War, Washington's debts equaled $240 million, down from an all-time high a few years before. Meanwhile, other countries' debts had risen, especially as economic *recession* hit the emerging economies of Eastern Europe, forcing such large payers as Russia and

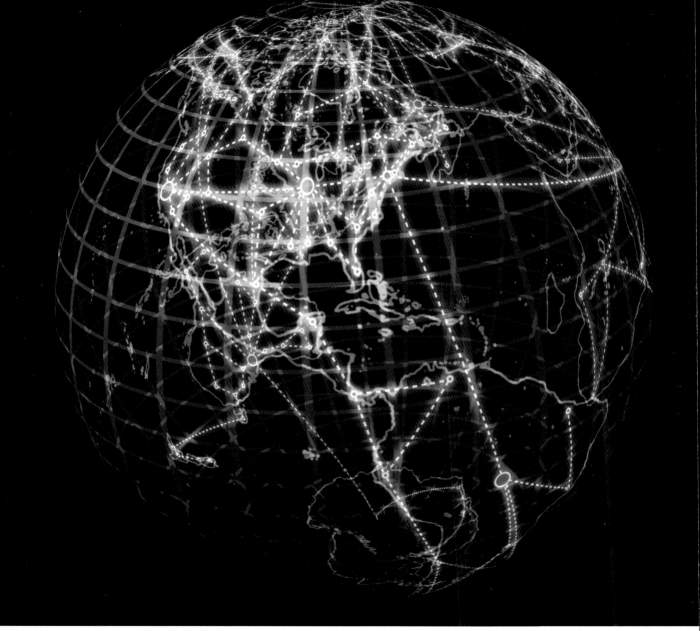

Internet communication spans the globe, which means an e-mail tax could yield considerable income for the United Nations.

Ukraine into massive debt. In 1992, while U.S. arrears had diminished, UN regular budget debts had grown to a record $501 million. The result was that the United States was now the UN's largest debtor, and the United Nations was, and remains today, on the verge of bankruptcy.

Although financing for UN programs has diminished, the work left to be done by the world's only international governing body has greatly increased. More than half the world's population of 6 billion lives in poverty, and 800 million people suffer from *chronic* malnutrition. Meanwhile, disease, economic instability, and armed conflict also threaten much of the world.

Alternative Sources of Funding

It seems inevitable that the United Nations will have to develop additional ways to generate revenue. Worldwide taxes on currency trade, *carbon emissions*, and arms trade could counter many crises while at the same time raising revenue. A UN study has estimated that about $150 billion per year is needed to meet its Millennium Development Goals, which include reducing the proportion of people living in extreme poverty and hunger by half, ensuring primary schooling for all children, and reversing the spread of HIV/AIDS, malaria, and other major diseases by 2015. Many different proposals have been made to help raise the necessary funds.

The foreign currency exchange market is the largest market in the world, with an estimated $1.9 trillion currency traded per day. This means that in less than one year, currency worth ten times the global gross domestic product is traded. Economists have examined the possibility of levying a tax on international monetary transactions as a means to generate revenue. A tax rate ranging from 0.005 to 0.25 percent could generate between $15 and $300 billion per year, which would go far to promote international peace and development.

A large body of research promotes the economic and environmental wisdom of energy taxes. Arguments in favor of such a tax rest on the assumption that free markets are unable to incorporate all of the relevant social costs of economic activity, including damage to the climate from fossil fuel emissions, into the end price of goods. Thus, the goal of an energy tax is to correct this by enabling the price of goods and services to reflect full social and environmental costs. Carbon taxes make the greatest sense because they tax emissions directly. Coal creates the greatest amount of carbon emissions and would therefore be taxed in greater proportion than oil and natural gas, which have lower carbon concentrations. This is also felt to be a fair way to impose a global tax because the tax would be passed on to individuals according to wealth, in direct proportion to the amount they consume.

An e-mail or Internet tax, also known as a "bit tax," seeks to introduce a tax on the amount of

The United Nations will need money if it is to promote peace and justice in the years to come.

data sent through the Internet. Because of the volume of data sent via e-mail, the tax could be very slight and still generate a tremendous amount of revenue. A person sending a hundred e-mails a day, for instance, each containing a ten-kilobyte document, would pay a tax of just one cent, according to one proposal. Proponents of such a tax hope to raise funds that would be spent to close the "digital divide" between rich and poor.

The UNDP Human Development Report 1999 researched such a tax. The UNDP estimated that globally in 1996, this type of tax would have yielded $70 billion. Since Internet users now frequently send data-rich photos and large documents, transfer rates are far higher than in 1996, while the number of Internet users has grown. For these reasons, a tax should be set at a rate well below the one UNDP first proposed. Still, it could produce a large boost to the UN's operating budget while impacting most users very little.

Looking Toward the Future

Many reforms are being made, both by the United Nations itself and by member nations to help end the serious financial crisis the organization faces. The United Nations is working to make the most out of every dollar it spends and to disclose its financial records more fully, giving those countries that fund the body more confidence that their money is being well spent. As the United Nations looks to the future, it is clear that there is much work to be done to promote peace and justice in the world.

Time Line

1815	The Holy Alliance is formed.
1825	The Holy Alliance is dissolved.
1864	The First Geneva Convention is adopted.
1914	World War I begins.
1919	Paris Peace Conference accepts Wilson's proposal to create the League of Nations. Treaty of Versailles signed.
1920	The first meeting of the League of Nations is held.
1926	Germany is admitted to the League of Nations.
1932	Japan withdraws from the League of Nations.
1933	Germany withdraws from the League of Nations.
1934	The Soviet Union joins the League of Nations.
1939	The Soviet Union is expelled from the League of Nations. World War II begins.
1945	World War II ends. The United Nations is founded.
1946	League of Nations dissolves itself, and all services, mandates, and property is transferred to the newly formed United Nations.
1963	Articles 23, 27, and 61 of the UN Charter are amended.
1965	Amendments to Articles 23, 27, and 61 take force.
1969	Amendment to Article 109 takes force.

1971	People's Republic of China replaces the Republic of China as China's representative to the United Nations.
1973	Second amendment to Article 61 takes force.
1991	Russia replaces the Soviet Union.
2005	Special session of the General Assembly is held to commemorate the UN's sixtieth anniversary.
2006	The United Nations continues to seek new ways to fund its programs.

Glossary

absolute monarchs: Royalty who have complete control over every aspect of their kingdom and subjects.

abstain: Not vote either for or against a proposal when a vote is held.

advocate: Someone who supports or speaks in favor of something.

alliances: Associations of two or more groups of people who work together to achieve a common goal.

amelioration: The act of improving something.

amendments: Changes or alterations to something.

appeasement: The political strategy of pacifying a potentially hostile nation in the hope of avoiding war.

arrears: Unpaid debts.

averting: Preventing something from occurring.

breach: Violation of an agreement.

carbon emissions: Pollution emitted from the burning of a carbon, such as coal.

chivalry: The combination of qualities expected of the ideal medieval knight, especially courage, honor, and loyalty.

chronic: Long term or frequently recurring.

collective security: The maintenance of peace and security through the united action of nations.

contention: Disagreement.

conventions: Agreements between groups, slightly less formal than a treaty.

decolonization: The process of granting a colony its independence.

delegates: Representatives with the power to act on behalf of another.

diplomats: Members of a government who represent their countries in dealings with other countries.

Eurocentric: Focusing on Europe, its people, institutions, and culture.

fascist: Someone who supports a system of government characterized by dictatorship, centralized control of private enterprise, repression of all opposition, and extreme nationalism.

gross domestic product: The total value of all goods and services produced within a country in a year, minus net income from investments in other countries.

humanitarian: Concerned with the well-being of others.

incumbent: Necessary as a result of duty, responsibility, or obligation.

lobby: Petition representatives on behalf of an issue.

memoirs: Written accounts of a person's life or the events in which he or she participated.

nationalism: An extreme sense of loyalty to one's country.

negotiation: The act of reaching an agreement through discussion and compromise.

neutrality: The state of not taking a position in a war or other conflict.

pacifist: Someone who holds the belief that violence, war, and taking lives are unacceptable methods of solving disputes.

pandemic: Existing in the form of a widespread epidemic that affects people in many different countries.

per capita income: The amount earned by each individual.

preamble: The beginning words of a speech, report, or document that explain the purpose of what follows.

precedent: An action or decision on which a future action or decision can be based.

prorated: Calculated, divided, or distributed something proportionally.

protocol: A formal agreement between states or nations.

ratified: Officially approved.

recession: A period of economic decline shorter in duration than a depression.

reparations: Compensations demanded of a defeated nation by the victor in a war.

resolutions: Formal expressions of the consensus at a meeting, usually arrived at by a vote.

sanctions: Rules or laws that lead to a penalty when disobeyed.

signatories: Those who have signed a treaty.

subsidiary: A company or organization controlled or owned by a larger one.

supersede: Take the place of something less efficient, less modern, or less appropriate.

tribute: Payment made by one ruler to another as a sign of submission.

Triple Entente: The 1907 alliance between the United Kingdom, France, and Russia.

universal validity: Complete agreement.

Further Reading

Edwards, Amy. *United Nations at Work: The Challenge of Building Global Peace.* Washington, D.C.: Close-Up Foundation, 1995.

Riggs, Robert E., Jack C. Plano, and Lawrence Ziring. *United Nations: International Organization and World Politics.* Belmont, Calif.: Wadsworth Publishing, 1999.

Ross, Stewart. *United Nations.* Chicago, Ill.: Raintree Library, 2004.

Tessitore, John. *Kofi Annan: The Peacekeeper.* Newark, N.J.: Scholastic Library Publishing, 2000.

Woog, Adam. *United Nations.* Farmington Hills, Mich.: Thomson Gale, 2004.

For More Information

Charter of the United Nations
www.un.org/aboutun/charter/index.html

Office of the President of the General Assembly
United Nations
New York, NY 10017
Tel.: (212) 963-7555
Fax: (212)963-3301
www.un.org/ga

United Nations Cyberschoolbus
www.un.org/Pubs/CyberSchoolBus/index.asp

United States Mission to the United Nations
140 East 45th Street
New York, N.Y. 10017
Tel.: (212) 415-4050
Fax: (212) 415-4053
www.un.int/usa

Publisher's note:
The Web sites listed on this page were active at the time of publication. The publisher is not responsible for Web sites that have changed their addresses or discontinued operation since the date of publication. The publisher will review and update the Web-site list upon each reprint.

Reports and Projects

Maps

• Make a map of the world, and indicate countries that have been the site of UN peacekeeping operations.

Reports

• Write a brief report on the League of Nations. What were its successes? What failures led to the creation of the United Nations?
• Research a resolution made by the Security Council. Describe the situation that brought the matter before the Security Council, and what action it took in response. Was the action of the Security Council effective?
• Write a report on one of the UN's primary organs and its function.

Biographies
Write a one-page biography on one of the following:

• Kofi Annan
• Woodrow Wilson

Group Activities
• Gather a group of friends and create a mock Security Council. Let some students represent permanent members and others the elected members of the council. Create a fictional conflict and work together to draft a resolution to take action against the country acting as the aggressor.

• Research the procedures of the General Assembly, and create a mock session of the General Assembly to discuss levying an e-mail tax to increase revenue. Have each student represent a different country and present their view of the tax. Which countries would likely support such a measure? Which countries would be against it?

Bibliography

The Avalon Project: Constitution of the United Nations.
　　http://www.yale.edu/lawweb/avalon/decade/decad049.htm.

Global Policy Forum. http://www.globalpolicy.org.

The Nobel Prize for Peace. http://www.nobelprize.org/peace.

United Nations. http://www.un.org.

U.S. Department of State. http://www.state.gov.

Index

Picture Credits

Corel: pp. 8, 15, 20, 22, 24, 26, 27, 28, 30, 35, 36, 37, 39, 40, 41, 42, 44, 46, 50, 54, 57, 58, 59, 60, 66, 67
iStock: p. 52
    Fred Minnick p. 71
    Lee Pettet p. 70
    Lisa Kyle Young p. 49
    Perry Kroll p. 72
Photos.com: pp. 64, 74
United Nations: p. 62
U.S. Army Center of Military History: p. 19

Biographies

Author

Heather Docalavich first became interested in the work of the United Nations while working as an adviser for a high school Model UN program. She lives in Hilton Head Island, South Carolina, with her four children.

Series Consultant

Bruce Russett is Dean Acheson Professor of Political Science at Yale University and editor of the *Journal of Conflict Resolution*. He has taught or researched at Columbia, Harvard, M.I.T., Michigan, and North Carolina in the United States, and educational institutions in Belgium, Britain, Israel, Japan, and the Netherlands. He has been president of the International Studies Association and the Peace Science Society, holds an honorary doctorate from Uppsala University in Sweden. He was principal adviser to the U.S. Catholic Bishops for their pastoral letter on nuclear deterrence in 1985, and co-directed the staff for the 1995 Ford Foundation Report, *The United Nations in Its Second Half Century.* He has served as editor of the *Journal of Conflict Resolution* since 1973. The twenty-five books he has published include *The Once and Future Security Council* (1997), *Triangulating Peace: Democracy, Interdependence, and International Organizations* (2001), *World Politics: The Menu for Choice* (8th edition 2006), and *Purpose and Policy in the Global Community* (2006).

88